FINDING MY VOICE
with *Aphasia*

FINDING MY VOICE
WITH *Aphasia*

Walking through Aphasia

CAROL M. MALONEY

iUniverse, Inc.
Bloomington

Finding My Voice with Aphasia
Walking through Aphasia

Copyright © 2013 by Carol M. Maloney.

All rights reserved. No part of this book may be used or reproduced by any means, graphic, electronic, or mechanical, including photocopying, recording, taping or by any information storage retrieval system without the written permission of the publisher except in the case of brief quotations embodied in critical articles and reviews.

iUniverse books may be ordered through booksellers or by contacting:

iUniverse
1663 Liberty Drive
Bloomington, IN 47403
www.iuniverse.com
1-800-Authors (1-800-288-4677)

Because of the dynamic nature of the Internet, any web addresses or links contained in this book may have changed since publication and may no longer be valid. The views expressed in this work are solely those of the author and do not necessarily reflect the views of the publisher, and the publisher hereby disclaims any responsibility for them.

Any people depicted in stock imagery provided by Thinkstock are models, and such images are being used for illustrative purposes only.
Certain stock imagery © Thinkstock.

ISBN: 978-1-4759-8669-3 (sc)
ISBN: 978-1-4759-8720-1 (hc)
ISBN: 978-1-4759-8670-9 (ebk)

Library of Congress Control Number: 2013907067

Printed in the United States of America

iUniverse rev. date: 05/07/2013

To my late mother and my Dad.
Thank you for being there for me and helping me through my stroke and for your continuing encouragement with my aphasia.

My first kiss and the flowerbed.
Your first puppy love is wonderful and never forgotten.
Thanks, Billy

CONTENTS

Part One   Life before My Stroke..................................1

Part Two   The Stroke 31

Part Three   Life after my Stroke......................................55

Lifesaving   Signs of a Stroke 71

Resources..73

PART ONE

LIFE BEFORE MY STROKE

"Girls, wake up! It is seven o'clock. Half the day is gone. We need to clean this house." T'was the Irish battle cry every Saturday morning. It did not matter that we cleaned the house every night before we went to bed. Saturday was a special cleaning day. On that day we polished furniture, washed windows, and cleaned the beloved crystal chandelier and the kitchen until every countertop, every leg of every table, and every chair was polished. The floors were washed and the rugs vacuumed. The two bathrooms, used by the seven of us, were scoured until they shined like the sun reflecting from the crystal chandelier. Dismissal time was three o'clock—only then could we go out with our friends. My mother was first-generation Irish and continued this tradition she had learned from her mother.

The tradition continued as I grew older and even after I left home in 1980. I always cleaned my home on Saturday morning. And I kept cleaning when I moved back home with my parents in 1998 to help my mother take care of Dad after cardiac surgery and never left. Mom passed away in 2007, and I continued the Saturday morning tradition. One Saturday morning in June 2009, I heard the "battle cry to clean the house," but little did I know this "battle cry" would become a cry for help—I had a stroke while cleaning the house.

EDUCATION

I graduated from a Catholic high school believing the only job I was capable of doing was waitressing. In my junior year my guidance counselor reported to my mother and I that she believed I was not capable of college-level work because I was extremely shy, had B-minus to C grades, and did poorly on my pre-SAT. The counselor believed college-level work would be too difficult for me, and therefore it would be a waste of time and money. Feelings of disappointment, discouragement, and failure overwhelmed me. My goal to be the first child in the family to graduate from college vanished with those words. My mother was furious at the counselor. She could not believe the counselor would express her beliefs in such a callous manner. My mother's response was, "We will see about that!" as she stormed out the counselor's office with me on her arm. We did not speak about it that night. The next day was Saturday and we cleaned the house, only this time in deep thought about those devastating words.

My senior year in high school I met Sister Rose Paula, who taught US history. She was kind but very strict. As the first few months of school went by, she realized my reading level was below average and my comprehension and ability to recall the material were poor, resulting in an inability to do well on the written test. Soon I was in her classroom taking a Stanford reading evaluation test. A few days later she told me that my reading and comprehension abilities were below average by several grade levels and that this was what had caused my frustration and poor grades overall. "We, my friend," she said, "are going to teach you to read." The next several months Sister Rose Paula and I stayed after school for my reading program. "Start with the basics and move to mastery" was our motto. Weeks later our hard work resulted in improved grades and better reading and comprehension skills. At the end of my senior year, my reading and comprehension were at grade level. Our hard work had paid off. Reading is a lifelong skill needed to succeed, and Sister Rose Paula gave me a new life. I graduated from high school prepared for my next challenge. Later in life I emulated Sister Rose Paula in my teaching.

My academic journey continued in September 1971 at Quincy Junior College in Quincy, Massachusetts. My goal was to prove to myself that I could be more than a waitress. No student should ever hear those stinging words, and therefore I set my sights on teaching. Quincy Junior College offered new life experiences for me. My sisters and I had been lovingly sheltered from the world. We had attended all-girl parochial schools and had experienced very little interaction with the outside world, including boys. But now I was entering the real world and a co-ed college, resulting in the social challenges of interacting with boys as well as individuals from different backgrounds and religions. It would be an understatement to say I was amazed that not everyone was Catholic.

I met my first love, Billy Handrahan, at Quincy Junior College. Puppy love is wonderful. I was enthralled by the experience of reciprocated, unconditional love. We met in the "Cave," or student lounge, in between classes in January 1972. He was playing cards, and I was studying for a history exam the next day. My new friends began teasing me about relaxing and invited me to watch the card game. When Billy and I looked at each other, my heart went into my throat, my face turned red, and I was speechless. Later that night we talked for hours on the phone, neither one of us willing to end the call first. I was in heaven. So this is what life is about, I thought. We were always together in school. However, our part-time jobs did not allow for dating. In our study group, I was the history and writing genius, Billy was the math genius, and Timmy was the economics genius. Unfortunately, we were not in the same history class but did have the same teacher.

In April we had midterm exams. We were as nervous as a cat in a room filled with rocking chairs. The exam was difficult and a little confusing. My morning exam allowed me to inform the others what to expect. That afternoon Bill came bursting into the Cave and then ran outside. I ran after him to find out what was wrong. He thought he had failed the exam. He was enraged, but I was able to de-escalate the situation. We went to have coffee before his bus was due. As we walked to the bus stop, I kept reassuring him he passed the test and "safe home." He smiled and thanked me for always being there for him. This is when I had my first kiss: at the post office stairs waiting for his bus. I was so surprised I fell into the flowerbed behind me. Graceful, I was not, but after he dug me out of the flowerbed, we laughed so hard, tears happily pouring down our very red cheeks. It was one of those "duh" moments. Everyone experiences them: you hit your head with your hand, saying to yourself, "What did I just do?" It was a moment that has stayed in my heart for years. It was a happy and loving moment and has helped me through some tough times. Later in life whenever I was overwhelmed, exhausted from caregiving, or having a bad day, I would think of that moment and smile. It re-energized me: a touching moment that would be with me, always.

Dr. Keogh, philosopher extraordinaire, was my counselor and lifeline in college. He was a remarkable teacher. He listened, offered insight, and taught me the study skills needed to deal with my workload. He believed, as did I, that it was ironic that I waitressed to help pay my way through college. I made the dean's list every semester. In May 1973, I graduated with honors from Quincy Junior College with my Associates Degree in liberal arts and social sciences. That day Colonel Robert Dean, my constitutional law teacher and a former attaché for General Eisenhower during World War II, told my parents I was brilliant and would be very successful. My mother cried when she heard those words. Mom and I worked hard together, and we had made it.

The sad part of graduating was that Billy went onto a military academy. Before he left, he arranged to have dinner at a Cape Cod country club. It was elegant. After dinner we walked along the beach, telling each other how we would write every day and call once a week. It was like a scene from a movie—everything was perfect. The following year, on his twenty-first birthday, his mother and I went to the military academy to visit him. Bill and I went out to dinner, and as we walked through the campus, he gave me a beautiful piece of jewelry—a mother-of-pearl heart with the inscription "Love as always." I still have it. Unfortunately, his military travels and our jobs caused us to part ways. But the memories will always be there.

My educational journey continued at Suffolk University in Boston, Massachusetts, where I studied secondary education and social studies. The student population was much larger, and required a higher quality of work. Oh boy! The initial days were confusing and frustrating. I was lost more than I could be found. The new juniors in each class compared schedules, and as a team, we overcame the task of finding our assigned buildings and classrooms. I needed a place to study, and my mother agreed to convert her beloved dining room into a study. For the next two years, when my study group came over, she served tea, Irish bread, and sweets as we studied. However, I had to clean the dining room and organize it every Saturday morning. During the holidays, we converted it back to a dining room. I moved my books and typewriter to my bedroom, polished the furniture and the chandelier, and cleaned the rug. In June 1975, I received my Bachelor of Science in secondary education and social sciences with honors. Graduation was held at the Hynes Memorial Auditorium. Mom and I did it. I was the first to graduate from college in my family. I proudly mailed my graduation announcement, along with the program indicating I had graduated with honors, to my high school guidance counselor. She never responded. I wonder why?

My life as a teacher began, or so I thought. Substitute teaching is not an ideal situation for teachers fresh out of college. Your classroom management skills are not yet developed, and often you are not teaching in your area of expertise. At the time the pay was twenty-five dollars a day, and the schedule was erratic. I was waiting near the phone every morning for the school to call. Meanwhile, I was sending out resumes and praying for an interview. I learned early that nepotism is the golden key to the education hiring system. Teaching is an innate ability, and just because you are the niece of an administrator does not automatically mean you can teach, especially without a college degree. I have seen too many good teachers be passed over for a job because an administrator's or school committee member's relative or friend (sometimes without the appropriate degrees and certification) needed a job. These relatives and friends could not control a classroom or teach if their life depended on it. The students suffer the most, which is just wrong!

EMPLOYMENT

Two years into an unsuccessful quest for a permanent teaching job I responded to an employment opportunity at a prestigious law firm in Boston. This was a very strange interview. I was asked to copy a page from the *Wall Street Journal*. The human resource director admired my handwriting and inquired about my interpersonal skills. Then I met with my new boss, the supervisor of the trust and estate tax department, and was hired that day. Catholic school had paid off—the reason I was hired was my clear and beautiful handwriting. I was disappointed that I was not teaching, though. I loved working with children and wanted to help them succeed the way Sister Rose Paula had helped me. I felt as though I had deserted my dream. I needed a job to pay student loans, pay bills, and just live. I worked as a fiduciary accountant and tax preparer. My responsibilities included collecting dividends and interest for each trust account and posting any stock transactions or trades, which were completed by the attorneys or trustees, into individual trust journals. I was held accountable for each client's money, which was usually more than $2 million. I had to do monthly and quarterly reports and send them to each client. The annual probate trust accountings had to be signed by the trustee or attorney and sent to our clients for approval and signature. After I had completed the annual trusts, I started on the tax preparation component. I prepared trust returns for each trust (543 to be exact). The final step of the process was preparing the individual tax returns for each client and beneficiary based on the trust information and individual tax information. Meanwhile I organized the individual tax information sent to me to complete each return. My other responsibilities included distributing monthly allowances from each trust account to the beneficiaries and payroll for domestic and nursing care. Ironically, my worst subject in school had been math. Thank God for calculators.

The law firm sent me to school to earn my master's degree in probate accounting and taxation in 1982, which resulted in a promotion to assistant trust and tax department supervisor. Each year from October through May 15, we filed 543 probate accountings, 600 trust tax returns, and over 700 personal income tax returns for our clients. Along with my regular duties, such as payroll for the domestic help, paying bills, and scheduling and paying private duty nurses for my clients, this meant fifteen- to eighteen-hour days.

I eventually had more interaction with clients. I was amazed to realize that several of the clients had changed the political course of United States history during World War II, were well-known philanthropists, or had made their money during the Second Industrial Revolution. There were some interesting people. One day I received a call from a home care provider asking me to come to a client's home immediately. Upon arrival, everything seemed in order. The home care provider requested I visit the bathroom. I was in complete shock. The client had found what she thought were just beautiful papers in her study and had decided to paper her bathroom walls with them. Unfortunately, the papers were Standard Oil of New Jersey stock—a.k.a. Exxon—with an estimated worth of $4.5 million. In retrospect, it was actually funny, but at the time, I was horrified.

I remained with the law firm for ten years. Each year after tax season the partners of my firm and I would take time off and go on vacation. I headed to my second home: the York Harbor Inn in York, Maine. I would call the York Harbor Inn well in advance to make reservations for a week in my favorite room. This would give me the boost I needed to get through the seemingly endless and miserable tax season. Once at the Inn I always received a warm welcome. The staff told me to get some rest, and to let them know if I needed anything. Can you say pampered?

In 1986, I was recruited by a moderate-size fiduciary firm in Boston. They had recognized my forte in trust accounting and taxes and offered a large wage increase that was almost doubled my current salary. I took the job and became supervisor of the trust and tax department. The changes in my responsibilities were exceptional: I became more involved in interpreting trust and estate documents and participated in filing the then-largest estate tax return with the Internal Revenue Service Northeast region. Surprisingly, we survived the audit without paying additional taxes. Most excitingly, we introduced computers in the office to expedite our workload, thus finally moving into the twenty-first century. The days of handwriting trust accountings and calculating trust and individual taxes were finally over. It was unbelievable. What would usually take weeks to prepare by hand, the computer completed over a single weekend. I would still double-check the computer output as I did my own accounting to make sure an entry was coded correctly, but that was a piece of cake. Yet something was still missing. I wanted to be a positive influence on a child's life.

I enjoyed my work, but something was missing deep inside me. I wanted to be in the classroom, and so, in 1991, I began teaching religious education on Saturday and Sunday mornings for an hour at my parish Saint Catherine of Siena. Nothing could replace the joy I felt when I interacted with children.

THE FIRE

January 16, 1996, was an extremely cold day. I arrived at the office at 6:30 a.m. to get an early start on the long day ahead. Little did I know my life was about to drastically change. My boss and I greeted each other and spoke about the weather and schedules. Were we on schedule with the trust accountings? When would we start the trust tax returns? We followed our routine and went into the kitchen to make coffee and tea. Suddenly the fire alarm went off, followed by an announcement telling us that it was a mistake and everything was fine. We went into our respective offices. While turning on my computer, I looked out my tenth-floor window and saw a large ball of fire explode through the fifth-floor window. I screamed. My boss came running into my office, and we looked at each other terrified. I was always told I was a workaholic and would die at my desk. But this was not the way I wanted to go. As we ran to the office entrance, the fire alarm sounded. We peered out the glass door and watched a dark fog heading toward us. Immediately I called the fire department and was told the building was on fire—no kidding, Dick Tracy—and was being evacuated. In my mind I was praying for them to hurry it along. The fifth floor was engulfed with fire; we were on the tenth floor.

"Let's get out of here! Let's go down the fire stairwell!" my boss and I said in unison. The stairwell was filled with heavy, black smoke. We attempted to go down anyway, but the heat and smoke forced us to retreat back up to the office. By then the office was also engulfed in gray smoke that quickly turned black. My boss opened the windows hoping for relief from the heat and suffocating smoke but with little result. The smoke had turned so black we could not see each other anymore. Panic chilled my body. He called my name, and when we finally found each other, we held hands attempting to calm each other, but also saying good-bye. All we could do was wait.

"Where are you?" came a voice out of nowhere. I was speechless, but my boss yelled out our location. My immediate reaction was to go where the ladder would likely be—out the window. Fresh air would fill my lungs and the burning pain in my throat and chest would be relieved. I wanted to be safe again. That day I learned that the tallest fire ladder in the city of Boston only reaches to the seventh floor. "What?" my boss and I said in unison. "You have to be kidding. How the hell are we getting out of here?" The firemen told us that we were going down the fire stairs they had climbed to get to us. I did not think it was possible; more panic went through my body. Bobby Culbert was my firefighter. He quickly but gently put a fire blanket around me, gave me some oxygen, and said we would be okay. Next he asked me to maneuver my way through the office toward the fire stairway. "The stairway with all the smoke? Are you crazy?" It seemed like a lifetime, but we finally got there. Before we descended those stairs, he said the words that scared the hell out of me. "We are going to share the oxygen going down the stairs. The fifth floor is engulfed in flames. So do not stop; just run like hell." I remember him pushing me onward until the heat was unbearable and my mind shut down.

The next thing I remember is hearing my name and wearing an oxygen mask. A soft voice was telling me that I was going to be okay and that I just needed to keep breathing normally. Thank God I was not dead. I arrived at the Massachusetts General Hospital with black soot on my face, hands, and every speck of skin that had been exposed. As they cleaned me up, I noticed that my skin was yellow and my throat and lungs were in unbearable pain. I could not speak. In my mind I wondered why I was yellow. As if the nurse had read my mind, she told me that this was caused by the smoke inhalation. "Medication and wide-open oxygen will take care of it. The X-rays showed some lung scarring, but luckily the burns will heal without scarring."

I was numb and did not show any emotion until my parents appeared at the door. Then my tears fell like Niagara Falls. As she administered medication, the nurse told me to think happy thoughts. Within minutes, I was dreaming about the flowerbed and my first kiss. I was released the next day. My parents wanted me to stay with them, but I went home to my condo in Nashua to snuggle up on my couch and cry. Suddenly I was more aware of exits and escape routes. My family doctor explained that it was natural for a fire survivor to experience these feelings and they would eventually stop. During the day, I did my trust accounting and taxes at home to keep me busy. I had arranged to have them delivered and picked up when they were finished, with new work being delivered at the time of the pickup. My doctor had given me a mild sedative for panic attacks and sleeping. He firmly urged me to go to the York Harbor Inn for the weekend, relax, read a book, and enjoy friends. So I did. As I drove to the Inn, I began to smell smoldering timbers—I thought someone had their fireplace working in one of the beautiful mansions across from the Inn right by the water. But to my surprise, as I arrived at the Inn I found the smoldering remains of the five beautiful mansions. What the hell happened? Did someone jinx me? When I checked in, I was told that Hartley Mason, who had owned the property, had died recently. His will stipulated that the houses be burnt to the ground and replaced with a park. The park was his gift of perpetuity to the people of York. The Inn had a spectacular water view. I returned home feeling better and more relaxed.

Six weeks later, the office had been renovated, and I went back to work. You could still smell hints of smoke along with the citrus chemical used to cover the odor. I immediately opened my window about an inch. The windows used to be sealed shut, which meant that during the fire we had to unseal them with a small jackknife and a letter opener to get some air. If, God forbid, there was another fire, the window would be open to allow for some fresh air. For several weeks, things went along smoothly: I was working late hours and sleeping better. My biggest problem was dealing with the complaints from my fellow employees about the opened window. They claimed they were cold, but I worked less than three feet away from the window and did not feel cold. I told them to put on a sweater or gloves. This was my little office and my window, so I told them to get over it: "I will even build you a bridge to get over it. Just stop complaining." I worked Saturdays, which markedly improved my productivity at work. The peace and quiet in the office was a blessing.

One Friday night in late February, my boss suggested I leave at six and come back in the morning fresh. I rode down the elevator thinking about what to make for supper, when suddenly the elevator jerked to a stop. I started smelling smoke. At first, I thought it was my imagination but soon realized I was in trouble. I called security, knowing he was going to tell me the bad news. The workers on the fifth floor had sparked a fire while repairing the electricity. The fire knocked out the electricity. *Oh God not again! I cannot do this again!* I thought as I sank to the floor of the elevator. I was numb with fear, chills running through my body. I fell into a world of disbelief, trying to convince myself that this was not happening again. I began thinking about my first kiss, Bill's crystal-blue eyes, and laughing as I fell into the flowerbed. *That did not work; to hell with the kiss! I just want to get out of here.* Preferably alive. I opened my eyes and realized I was reliving my nightmare all over again. The smoke became thicker and thicker. I wrapped my scarf around my face and prayed. Smoke inhalation is going to kill me, I thought. As my lungs began burning from the smoke, I prayed to God: "Please help me make it." Suddenly, the loud sound of steel banging against the doors brought me back to my senses: the doors were being opened by the Jaws of Life. The best sound I ever heard. I covered my head and suddenly heard Bobby Culbert's familiar voice saying, "You will be all right. Take my oxygen mask." Two firefighters lifted me out of the elevator and gave me more oxygen. In disbelief, I said to Bobby, as tears flowed down my face, "Thank you, but I never want to see you again." He shook his head in agreement. My travels down the smoke-filled stairs began again; Bobby and I shared his oxygen mask. I arrived at the Massachusetts General Hospital around seven thirty, where I was treated for smoke inhalation, again, and thankfully sent home. My doctor called that evening, checking in on me and telling me to take the sedative he had prescribed earlier. I had a reputation for not taking medication, especially sedatives. We made an appointment to meet Monday morning.

Restlessness and vivid details of both fires overtook my mind all night. The fear, the smell of smoke; the panic; being stuck in the elevator; running down the stairs; and my body burning from the heat—I woke up screaming and soaked in sweat several times. I took showers for relief, only to have the dreams reoccur when I went back to sleep. I was exhausted but drove to Boston the next day to visit my doctor. I was glad his office was on street level. As I told him about the vivid dreams of the fire that kept me awake at night, the concern on his face grew. *This is not good.* He prescribed a mild sedative to be taken three times a day and told me to take a few weeks off until the nightmares stopped. Obediently, I took the prescribed sedative that night, but the nightmares began again, this time adding a new angle—how to escape a fire in my home? I needed a plan to escape my home if it was on fire. I timed my escape routes: eighteen seconds from my bedroom to the front door. My condo was in a gated community with security guards on patrol, but they were not prepared to fight a fire. I went to the living room—which had the floor-to-ceiling slider doors—opened them, and tried to sleep on the couch. I would be safe on the coach. The doors were open, allowing me to get out in five seconds—my fastest time. At last I was able to dose into a quiet sleep, dreaming about my fist kiss and the flowerbeds.

"What the hell are you doing? It's thirty-four degrees outside! Are you all right?" roared the security guard. "I bet it's hot flashes from menopause," said his sidekick, laughing. *Oh, go to hell, you idiot*, I thought, but out loud I simply told them to please leave me alone. They agreed only if I kept the sliding doors closed. *Yeah right, anything you say; just get out of here.* They left and five minutes later I opened the doors slightly and went back to sleep on the couch. I'd be able to get out in five seconds. But nonetheless, the nightmares engulfed my sleep again.

Walking was supposed to help with my symptoms. Realizing I had not been shopping since the elevator scare, I walked to Market Basket to replenish the food supply. I experienced something similar to an earthquake as I entered the store: my heart pounded, water trickled down my face, the store began to spin, and I could not find the exit. A lovely young girl passing by asked if I needed help. In a soft, quivering voice I told her I needed to find the exit. "It is right behind you," she answered and kindly walked me outside. What was wrong with me? What caused the panic attack? I needed answers.

The debilitating nightmares lingered for two weeks, as did my inability to enter a building. My primary-care doctor diagnosed me with post-traumatic stress disorder because I had developed more severe symptoms after the second fire. He decided that the next course of action was the post-traumatic stress disorder therapy at the Massachusetts General Hospital. What? I was not in Vietnam; I was in a bloody fire. Friends who survived the war suffered from PTSD. This did not make any sense. After checking in, I was told to take the elevator to the sixth floor. I stepped into the elevator only to have my body go into panic mode; I couldn't breathe, sweat poured down my face, and I began to smell smoke. I quickly stepped out. I entered the elevator again but with the same reaction. I found the stairs after realizing that a great number of employees have no idea where the stairs are located. Climbing the stairs was frightening, but I had climbed down ten flights of stairs to safety before. Climbing these stairs was the way to recovery and, hopefully, normalcy.

Tova Mueller, a post-traumatic stress expert, entered my life that day. She had long, blonde hair and was very tall and thin. The moment I met her, an aura of calmness and peace overcame me. Reassuringly, she ushered me into her office, telling me where all the exits were. We spoke about the fire, my nightmares, and the overwhelming fear of entering any building. She listened to me, gently touching my hand as I cried. "You and I will overcome these issues," she said softly but sternly. "It will take a lot of work, but I won't let you give up. Understood?" She was an angel. She didn't tell me to just get over it, a phrase I had heard many times before. She realized something else was bothering me. I told her that since the elevator fire I'd found myself disassociating from myself especially if I was afraid. She knew I was not crazy, but she knew my secret. She knew I had learned to shut the world out in my mind and was terribly afraid I could not bring myself back to reality. The phenomenon was called "skimming." Skimming is the world of the surreal; it is a safe place without panic; it is similar to feeling numb where nothing can hurt. She assured me it was a normal symptom of PTSD and she could help me.

Tova introduced me to coping skills. She taught me how to stimulate one of my five senses. For example, holding ice disengages you from skimming. My therapy included desensitizing my fear of fire and smoke. Each session included reliving every detail of the first fire until I could tell the story without emotions. We discovered that my trigger for PTSD was smoke. At the end of each meeting I received an assignment.

My first assignment was to visit Market Basket, find the exits, and stay in the store for one minute. I continued to do this every day, increasing the time until I felt comfortable. Within three months of therapy twice a week, I actually went grocery shopping. My feelings of accomplishment were beyond any words to express. My coping skills included finding the exits in every restaurant, store, or building I entered; staying on a comfortable-level floor in a hotel, then counting the paces and doors from my room to the exit both to my right and left; exiting a building immediately when an alarm sounds; and finally, always thinking toward the future, because the past can never be changed nor be relived.

During our sessions, I mentioned I had had several miscarriages yet had never felt closure. The baby blankets and clothes I had knitted for them were still in my bottom bureau drawer, wrapped in a white cloth. My maternal grandmother, Nana, acknowledged my pain: I could not have children. That knowledge was excruciating. In 1990, Nana had been diagnosed with cancer, suffering for many months. Several days before she died, her grandchildren visited to say good-bye. When I visited her, we spoke about how good she had been to me, and how I would miss talking with her over tea and Irish bread. I told her I loved her. As I was walking away, she touched my hand and said, "I will take good care of your babies. Don't worry." Tears filled my eyes.

Tova and I scheduled a memorial Mass for Nana and my babies in lieu of the next meeting. It was held in the chapel at the Massachusetts General Hospital on a Saturday afternoon. On the altar were white candles for each unborn child and two white teddy bears. One had a blue ribbon around its neck, the other a pink one. Tova sent an arrangement of white roses for the altar. During Mass, Tova suggested I envision Nana surrounded by my babies—it was beautiful. I cried for Nana and the babies. The closure I had been seeking for many years was found. Thank you, Tova, for understanding. You are an angel.

I retreated to my second home, the York Harbor Inn in York, Maine, for the tranquility and peace it offered. The spectacular ocean views and the rhythm of the waves at night rocked me to sleep. It was exactly what I needed. The friendship, caring, and genuine concern of the staff was overwhelming. In all my travels, my experiences at the Inn have never been surpassed. At the Inn I realized that teaching was my missing dream but I had done nothing to achieve it. Now, having faced death twice, I understood it was my destiny. Dear God, I had been given enough hints. I got it.

TEACHING—MY MISSING LINK

The fiduciary firm where I worked agreed to part ways, albeit with some animosity. The office was on the tenth floor, and I was unable to take the elevator, which I thought meant I could work at home. The firm's response was to get over it. They sent me flowers the next day. *You know what you can do with the flowers, don't you?* I thought. I was furious with the building management for not informing people about shutting off the sprinkler system and had little difficulty expressing my feelings. Over seven hundred people were working in the office building; imagine if the fire had started during regular working hours. Many people could have lost their lives or been seriously injured. It was appalling, but I found out that the upper management of each company in the building, including my boss, knew this and had received a reduced rent during the renovations. They made the choice not to inform their employees. In the end, the owners of the building were charged with over 250 building code violations. The goddamn money was the cause of my injuries.

My next venture in life was to work on being happy. After many hours of hesitation, I decided to work toward my dream. I had received my teaching degree from Suffolk University in 1975, and upon receiving my Master's degree in probate accounting and taxation in 1982, I taught seminars in trust accounting throughout my twenty years in probate accounting, which always gave me a sense of accomplishment. In spring of 1996 I timidly went to Rivier College in New Hampshire to pick up informational materials about their education courses. I also needed to know which credits could be transferred, and if there was other red tape I needed to cut. As I was looking at the materials, an older gentleman inquired what I needed. Tears came to my eyes and he invited me into his office. Dr. Mitsakos, Dean of the School of Education, reassuringly spoke with me about the process. We spoke about my prior employment, the fire, and my desire to teach. Leaving his office, I finally had a plan. I was admitted into the master's program in secondary-education studies in the social sciences. My first class started in mid-June 1996, and I graduated in 1998. Meanwhile I became a substitute teacher at Lowell High School enjoying every minute. Tova agreed it was a great idea, and told me, "You are on your way to achieve your lifelong goal." I loved learning and made many friends with an equal desire to teach. It was perfect. Dr. Mitsakos was my mentor and guiding light throughout my years at Rivier. His door was always open to me—for a problem; for encouragement when I was ready to give up; but mostly as a good friend. He is the epitome of a great teacher.

Teaching made me feel the best I had ever felt in years. I loved my students and I loved working with them. I worked in a vocational technical school in northeast Massachusetts. The school sat on sixty-eight acres and offered twenty-nine technical programs. The population was diverse, with over 90 percent of students living in the inner city. About two thousand students attended the school, and approximately 25 to 30 percent of them needed special-education. The schedule alternated a week in technical studies and a week in academics. Calling the first academic Monday challenging is a gross understatement. Social studies can be boring, and my job was to make it interesting. I usually taught between 260 and 290 students over a two-week period, and I was determined to teach my students to improve their reading and writing skills. It was interesting and exciting.

Ironically, while I was in probate law, we pressured the Massachusetts Department of Education for a standardized test as a requirement to graduate from high school. I was now on the other side of the coin—my job was to prepare them for the test my former colleagues and I had demanded as a graduation requirement. Experience taught me that reading and writing were the abilities most job applicants were lacking, and therefore these skills became an integral part of my social studies curriculum. What goes around comes around.

My teaching career began when I was forty years old. One of the veteran teachers became my mentor, although I was assigned to work with another teacher who was suffering from cancer. I was older and more mature than other teaching interns, and as a result, the school assumed I could handle more responsibilities for Mr. G. Basically I was thrown into the deep end of the pool without a life jacket. Mr. G was a wonderful man with a very dry sense of humor. He was also a revered former coach. His students adored him. His teaching style was no-nonsense—just learn the material and pass the test. But he also added humor to his methods. In the middle of a lecture he would stop and tell a joke or a humorous story. The kids loved it. Meanwhile, some of the veteran teachers thought I was just going through a midlife crisis and would not last long. People even made bets on how long I'd stick it out. They lost a lot of money. I was there for the long run.

Respect, humor, and teaching—that was my motto. We needed to earn mutual respect for each other; humor can be used to de-escalate most situations, and it can be utilized to make a fifty-minute history class less boring. My teaching philosophy was to use students' prior knowledge as a foundation and scaffold the information to history. Every day I wore a suit to class with heels—both students and faculty members called it my uniform. When asked why I wore these clothes, my response was: "Out of respect for you." On the first day of school, we discussed the rules and accountability. I set the bar of mastery, and it was their responsibility to meet it. I never let up on it, but I was always there to help them achieve mastery. Knowing my students was imperative; I needed to know their reading and comprehension levels and their favorite sport or activity. I requested reading and comprehension test scores as well as their state assessment scores. Reviewing them allowed me to modify the curriculum based on their abilities.

Protecting them and giving them a safe haven was a necessity. Within two weeks I met all my students. As they came in, I shook their hands. I invited them to a breakfast club, whereupon the students could take a quiet corner and finish their homework or talk to me about anything. Some students who were not even in my class would come in just for the food or to avoid being bullied before class. What was said in my classroom stayed in my classroom. Whoever broke this rule was no longer invited. The students requested a lunch club, which began at 11:30 a.m. The students would complain about the teachers or the detention they received. We would do what we called a social autopsy, and discuss why they received the detention and whether there was a better way to handle the situation in the future. Meanwhile others would sit, eat, and relax without being bullied. Soon it was clear that if someone bothered one of my kids, this someone had to deal with me. At 2:05 in the afternoon school was dismissed, except for the students who did not pass in their essays, failed a test, or needed to study for a makeup, as well as students who received detention but needed to learn the dynamics of reading and essay writing. At one point, students who received detentions from other teachers were allowed to come to my classroom to serve their detention. We reviewed reading skills and wrote or corrected essays. I served candy as I walked around helping students. I loved the interaction with them. Each afternoon there would be at least twenty to thirty-five students in my classroom. It felt as if Sister Rose Paula was reincarnated. I really wanted to help those poor kids.

Soon after I started teaching I was asked to write curriculum for my content area. It became my cornerstone in school. Instead of using the textbook three to four levels above their average reading level, I could develop a curriculum that was more appropriate for this specific student population and integrate reading, comprehension, and writing. I was in heaven.

In July 2002, I was accepted to the Gilder Lehrman Institute of American History at Columbia University in New York for a summer course in a new type of curriculum called Document Based Question, which used historical documents to teach history. I was in utopia surrounded by colleagues who shared common theories and strategies. I wanted to help my students more, so in 2002, I enrolled in the Certificate of Advanced Graduate Studies in Adolescent Literacy and Learning at Rivier

College. My dissertation was on improving adolescent reading and writing resulting in a comprehensive summer reading program. My students thought I was nuts as I introduced the document-based question program in the beginning, but they realized it could be interesting and fun. They had little self-esteem and confidence in their work, and the change in our routine made them uncomfortable. Fortunately, once they became familiar with the work, they actually enjoyed it. Rumor had it that some faculty members believed I was teaching at Princeton because of my notes and the themes I taught, but alas, they realized I set the bar high and my students met it. There was no option. If you could not meet the bar, then work after school was needed until you met the bar of mastery. No excuses. No exceptions.

Simplifying the content to their experiences and scaffolding to the objective of the day makes it easier for the student to follow. I introduced the curriculum I developed, "The Causes of War," by using their prior knowledge of gangs. I would ask the students the names of gangs in their neighborhoods and write them on the board. Then I asked them hypothetical questions about what causes gangs to fight. Turf became territory or imperialism. Gang colors become nationalism. Gangs joining together to avoid a take over or a war became alliances. On Monday, the students were put into groups of four to create a rap about the murder of the Archduke Ferdinand, which ultimately caused World War I. On Thursday they performed their raps to music and dancing. The best rap was selected in each class, and on Friday, "Miss M," as they called me, would perform the best six raps dressed as a gangsta. And so, Friday morning I was leaving the house in my baggy black pants, untied sneakers, two T-shirts, and about one pound of gold hanging from my neck along with rings on both hands. Thank God for Wal-Mart. Oh, did I mention that I also wore a hat and looked silly? I was living at home with my parents—we were taking care of each other. When they saw me on Friday morning, they gave me a look that clearly said, "Don't you dare go out like that." But I did. My routine was to stop at a coffee shop in Lowell before school; I was playing the rap music in the car, practicing my routine. When I entered the coffee shop, several of my kids were there. "Yo dog, hos it going," I'd say to greet them. The kids laughed so hard they were crying when I left. As I did my hallway duty, students walked by totally stunned and speechless. When the dean walked by and told me to take my hat off, because hats are not allowed in the building, my response was: "Stuff it." The students all applauded, and I immediately apologized for my rude behavior and took my hat off.

Columbia was a petite young girl with a great personality. She was born in Colombia and insisted on being called by that name. Despite her size, she was a firecracker on the basketball court. With help from Columbia, we performed my raps to the amazement and laughter of my students. Can you say feeling like a fool? During classes and lunch, I had over sixty students as well as teachers watching me in my classroom. It was a great day, and the icing on the cake was that every student received 90 percent or higher on the World War I exam.

I loved teaching. It consumed my entire life for fourteen years. I had finally found the missing piece of life. The kids and I had fun, but they also learned the content. In unorthodox ways, maybe, but it worked.

The most rewarding moment for a teacher is when a former student, who is now a junior, greets you with, "Hey, Ms. M.,

I passed the English language arts MCAS Exam. I wrote on the *Butterfly* play." Even students who positively despised me would come by and thank me. "Ms. M., I went on an interview and acted like you taught us and I got the job. Thanks." The most touching moment was when my mother died, and over thirty current and former students drove fifty miles (when I moved home in 1998, I traveled 104 miles roundtrip to school and home) to share their condolences at my mother's wake. I was overwhelmed with emotion and so proud of those students. I realized then that I was making a small difference.

PART TWO

THE STROKE

UNKNOWN FEELINGS

Mom died in 2007. Dad and I kept living together "to take care of each other," as he says. My mother's illness and painful death drained him. In 2004 Mom had been diagnosed with carcinoid cancer, a very rare and painful cancer—only one in eight million is stricken with this cancer. After three years and ninety-five days of round-the-clock care, she died in 2007. Dad and I were her main caregivers. When I came home from school, I would take care of her to give Dad a rest. Dad was very loving and caring. They had been married fifty-eight years, and facing her slow demise was very difficult. My sisters would call every night and visit to do their caregiving. Uncle Tim and Aunt Pat, Mom's brother and sister, visited and were always there for us. Our neighbors, Mary and Danny, would prepare food while Mom was in the hospital and keep an eye on both my parents while I was at school. Mary visited almost every day. They didn't know, but they were my rock that helped me keep it together. I was afraid that if I gave in to my emotions, I would accidentally prepare the medicines incorrectly or draw too much or too little medication into the syringes I prepared every night for the next day.

Hospice entered our home September 1, 2007. The reality of her death struck me hard. The Tuesday before she died I was told to stop all medications. I refused, and hospice called my mom's oncologist. He told me that it was her time. I cried for the first time in three years. She slipped into a coma on Thursday night and died Saturday at 4:32 in the afternoon, while Mass was being said for her. After her death, my father developed more cardiac issues, and we decided that I would continue to live with him. It was the best decision for both of us. Living with him I could save money to continue my studies. I had earned my postgraduate degree in the early stages of my mother's illness and began working on my PhD in adolescent literacy while living with Dad.

School was coming to an end, which meant the workload doubled: correcting final exams, helping my kids catch up on their work, and preparing report cards. It was a long week, but after fourteen years of teaching, you get used to it. It was eight o'clock on Saturday morning, June 9, 2009. I awoke to my father's familiar roar: "Get up, girl. Half the day is gone. Breakfast is on the table." It was a beautiful Saturday morning. My mother had been gone two years, but I thought of her especially on Saturdays. Dad went food shopping and I cleaned the house. I had been light-headed when I got up; I had a headache and just felt out-of-sorts. I attributed it to the heat, humidity, and the end-of-the-year schoolwork. As Dad and I ate breakfast, I felt better and decided to take a shower and do the Saturday cleaning as I had done since I was a little girl. Dad would be home by noon and I would go for my Saturday afternoon manicure. Life was simple. While in the shower I noticed that my sensations were not the same. I had to deliberately make my movements and think about where the soap and shampoo were located. My routine was disjointed; there was no fluidity. I held on to the safety bar as I got out of the tub. More questions began. *Where are the towels? Where is the comb and hair dryer? What in God's name is wrong with me?* I slowly and deliberately finished getting dressed. As I was walking out of the bathroom, I noticed my equilibrium and coordination were off. I thought I was coming down with a bug, and so, naturally, I made a cup of tea—an Irish tradition. It cures the worries of the world, my Nana would have said.

I started to feel better and decided to only do a quick house cleaning: just a quick dusting and vacuuming. As I was cleaning, the symptoms progressively became worse. My head was pounding and my right eye hurt. Was I experiencing a migraine? *What do I do?* Suddenly I had this unusual feeling of dissociation come over me. Was I skimming? I had not done that for years. No, this was not skimming; it felt totally different. I gingerly stumbled to the kitchen table and realized my cognitive functions were slowly diminishing. I could not think of my sister's telephone number. I had spent all my life working with numbers from trust accounting and taxes to correcting and grading papers. How could I forget a telephone number? It's those stupid cell phones; nobody remembers telephone numbers anymore. I forgot where I was. I could not identify anything on the kitchen table. Suddenly my right arm, face, and leg became tingly. When I came back from this disassociated feeling, I thought, *Oh my God, I am having a stroke. I need to call the police.* The problem was I could not find the phone. Vulnerability and isolation engulfed me. *Why isn't my brain working? Why is everything in slow motion? What is happening to my brain?* My body felt heavy and motionless. My mind felt like a tornado had just hit. I was weak as a kitten and so tired. I just wanted to take a nap. *I need to finish the curriculum I am writing. My students need it to pass the MCAS. Why am I so tired? Oh, I am losing myself again. I am skimming. Please let me come back.*

My Dad returned from grocery shopping to see me slouched over the kitchen table. He looked at my distorted face. In my mind, I asked him who my doctor was, but he did not understand me. *My voice is gone. My interpersonal skills and communicating skills are gone. I can't verbalize my problem. Mom had a stroke; she knew what it was like. I need to talk to her. I have worked so hard to become a teacher and now I cannot talk. Oh my God.*

My Dad called 911 and the ambulance finally arrived. They kept asking me questions and I tried to answer, but only unintelligible sounds came out. They told my Dad I was having a stroke and they were taking me to the local hospital. Suddenly nurses and doctors were talking to me. "Squeeze my hand; do you have any pain; how long ago did this start? Have you ever experienced this before? Can you move your hand? Please sign here." *Are you crazy? I have a big problem here and it is not getting any better. Stop shining that light in my eye. Could everyone stop talking at the same time? What is wrong with you people? Just slow down and give me a moment. For Christ's sake, just be quiet. A painkiller would be a good idea!* These thoughts ran through my mind, but I could not answer their questions. They took me for a CT scan of my brain and then an MRI. I knew what they were going to find that I was having a stroke or transient ischemic attack. I had watched my mother suffer a stroke, and the similarities were frightening. There were indications that my left temporal lobe was damaged. *Oh boy, I'm in trouble.*

The doctors explained to my Dad that a stroke occurs when a blood vessel in the brain bursts or, more commonly, when a blockage develops. Without treatment, cells in the brain quickly begin to die. My stroke or TIA affected the functions of the left temporal lobe. This affected comprehension, reading, articulation, and other language functions. Broca's area is one of the main areas of the cerebral cortex responsible for producing language. This brain area controls motor functions involved with speech production. Persons with damage to Broca's area of the brain can understand language but cannot properly form words or produce speech. Broca's area is located in the lower portion of the left frontal lobe. My Dad's response was: "For Christ's sake, speak English. What is wrong with her?" *Just tell me if I am going to live. What will happen next? Stop asking me questions. I am so tired,* I thought and drifted off into my place of tranquility. They told my Dad I had a stroke or TIA with residual effects of right-sided weakness with possible speech and comprehension deficits. They would not know the extent of these effects without further testing.

That night I was prodded and poked, blood was taken every couple of hours, and vital signs were taken every hour on the hour. Nurses came in to talk to me and perform neurological exams, telling me I was doing better. I would be a millionaire if I had a nickel for every time I was given a neurological exam in the first forty-eight hours of my admission. Their attitudes were positive, but their body language was cautious at best. Lisa, a wonderful nurse, was always asking me if I needed anything. "Are you warm enough? Do you need pain medication? Can I fix your pillows?" When food arrived, she came in to help me. She was a safe place for me. "Rest is what you need. Think of what makes you smile and get some sleep." She gave me some medication, and I drifted off, thinking about my first kiss and the flowerbed. I could not tell you where it happened or who it was, but it made me smile.

The next morning my condition improved in some but not all areas. I was disappointed but realized it was better than no improvement at all. The doctor, nurse, physical therapist, and speech therapist visited. They wanted to discuss their plan. They told me I had a TIA resulting in right-sided weakness and aphasia. *What the hell is aphasia? Can I take medication for it?* I just looked at them. "Good, we are all in agreement, and we will start with the plan tomorrow," said the doctor. *What? When did we develop a plan?* I did not understand most of what he said and was unable to respond, but I trusted he knew what he was doing. They left and I lay there, praying to Mom to make this a nightmare I could wake up from.

That afternoon a doctor came in and asked me all types of questions. "Where are you? What day is today? Who is the president of the United States?" I was unable to answer the questions, because I would only understand one word, and once I got that figured out, I tried to put a sentence together, but I could not focus. It was an effort and extremely tiring to focus on that person and put together an answer. By the time I had the answer, the doctor had moved on to other questions. All this left me confused. *Please stick to one question and give me time to answer it. My mind and mouth are not in sync. Just stop asking rapid-fire questions. Be patient and I will answer the first question. Give me some time to answer. I will find the words.*

Later on I would learn that stroke-survivor issues include the inability to think clearly; the inability to focus; diminished word-finding and socialization skills; short term and long-term memory loss; acute breakdown of communication; poor organizational skills; and diminished reading and comprehension abilities. The voices in your head—reminding you who you are, where you live, and what you are—fall silent. I was a lost soul with no perception or memory or emotion. All this was incomprehensible.

Lisa, my nurse, came in after the doctor left, and I pointed to my head and then to my mouth. "I know you know the answers," she said, thus telling me she knew what I was trying to say. "I know you wanted to say something but could not verbalize it. That is aphasia." She went on to tell me that it would be very frustrating but speech therapy would make it better. I felt like I was talking on the walkie-talkie in school with scratchy reception. I strained to hear what was being said, but I just could not understand. This was the most frustrating and patience-draining experience.

The third day my headache was almost gone and my right arm was not as numb. With help from the physical therapist, I sat up and took a few steps. Within minutes, I realized my stamina was gone. I felt weak, almost limp. I was disappointed as I crawled back into bed. I began to realize my primary-care doctor was right. "Listen to your body, and sleep when you need to. Sleep is the healing power of the body."

Peggy, my speech pathologist, visited me the next day. Her first concern was my swallowing. She asked me to drink, watching the motions of my throat. She asked me if I had problems eating, and I shook my head no. She spoke about my inability to communicate. Again I pointed to my head and then my mouth. The information was there in my mind; it just would not come out. "You have aphasia," she said. *Aphasia. Can it be cured? Is it permanent? Let's start to fix it.* She gave me some information on aphasia to read. Aphasia is a loss or reduction of language following brain damage, typically as a result of a stroke. This includes talking, understanding, reading, and/or writing. It is an acquired language problem, caused by damage to the brain in the hemisphere responsible for communication. Aphasia affects all modes of expressive and receptive communication including speaking, writing, reading, understanding, and gesturing. The extent to which these functions are affected depends on the location in the brain where the stroke occurred and the size of the stroke. Cognition, how we acquire language, as well as communication, the use of language, are the underlying processes that may be affected in aphasia. Some people may recover completely, while others may have permanent speech and language difficulties of varying degrees. *Oh my God. This is horrifying; what am I going to do? Teaching is all about expressive language. What is going to happen to me?* On the blackboard in my classroom I would usually write, "Silent and listen have the same letters." I used this phrase as a tool to keep my kids focused. I would point to it as a cue to be quiet and listen to me. If they disregarded my cue, they either had to go to detention or write an essay on being respectful.

Physically, I was making terrific progress. I gained my stability quickly, could get in and out of bed without help and could walk the hallway without much help except a cane. My primary-care doctor knew I was not happy about the cane, and his response was: "Don't be vain; use the cane." My arm was feeling better, and I could exercise my hand with the putty the physical therapist gave me. I was very happy with myself. Now I had to work on my brain. I realized I was not the same person and had a lot of work to do, but I felt I had the energy needed to tackle the aphasia. The new circuitry of my brain was different, but I could make the appropriate modifications.

On the fifth day, I came home. I was using a cane to compensate for my right-sided weakness, but with help from Dad and our neighbors Mary and Danny, I eventually made it up the stairs and into the house. Fortunately, the house is a seventy-foot ranch with the physical therapy equipment my mother had used during her illness. Maggie, my golden retriever, greeted me, her tail wagging. Maggie instinctively knew I was not feeling well, and she gently put her body next to mine for her usual belly rub. She never left my side. We shared the couch when I took a nap. I was on one end, and she curled up on the other. When I was getting up, she ran and retrieved my Dad. "Are you all right? Stay there; I'll help you up." Maggie stood in the doorway wagging her tail as if to say, "I'll watch over you." She is a wonderful companion for Dad and me.

Suddenly the doorbell rang. It was Mary, delivering dinner. Mary, Danny, and their boys are the epitome of good neighbors. While my mother was sick, she would visit on a regular basis and always bring goodies. She fed us during my mom's hospital stays, leaving a note on the refrigerator: "Chicken is in the fridge. Just microwave it for five minutes." Her sweets are the best. The boys, Luke, Greg, and Johnny, were always available to help. They would visit my mom or me consistently, asking if we needed anything. The boys range in age from six to fifteen, but they already have the social skills of very well-mannered young men. Of course, Mary and Danny are their role models, so what more can be said? There are no words to express my gratitude for all they have done for my family.

As rehabilitation began, I quickly learned I was in control of the success or failure of my treatment. I was at the crossroads—would I show up or give up? I found that the professionals who could look me in the eye, speak slowly and clearly, and had a gentle connecting touch were the ones I was willing to work with. A positive attitude was a key component too. Peggy had all these and more great qualities.

Peggy and I met three times a week to improve my speech. She told it the way it was. It was going to take a lot of work, and the results may not be normal as I knew it, but things would be better. I had to be willing to try—that was most important. Churchill's phrase, "Never, never, never give up," had a whole new meaning to me.

Dad was the key to my recovery. He was very understanding and patient, listening carefully when I was trying to tell him something. Actually, he became very good at charades. His favorite sayings were, "It could be worse," and, "I never met a quiet woman before," or, "At least you can keep a secret." He was very supportive and positive. And he drove me to all my doctor's appointments. "How the hell many doctors do you go to, girl?" He also drove me to Chris, my hairstylist. My mother and father loved Chris. Mom had been his client for over thirty years. She referred to him as the son she never had. The feeling was mutual.

Rehabilitation was difficult but also interesting. Focusing was my first challenge. My mind was buzzing with thoughts and feelings at warp speed. I would start a thought, and before I could finish it, I was already on a completely different thought. Unfortunately, the inability to focus impedes the other functions of the brain: speaking, understanding, reading, and writing. To maintain focus in rehabilitation, I initially scratched lines on a piece of paper for every word I spoke, and I then advanced to an exercise/squeeze ball to maintain my focus. Finally, I learned to use my hand as a metronome to focus and to speak.

Recognition cards—identifying pictures of everyday objects including pencils, animals, and different-shaped objects—were very difficult. Listening to words and then attempting to make the same sounds was beyond frustrating. Repetition was the key to maintaining focus. Peggy gave me a piece of paper and a pencil and instructed me to draw a line for each syllable. At first I could not do it. Then she instructed me to draw a line for each word in my mind. I had to continue doing this at home all the time. The third session was fantastic. I could draw the line and respond with a simple one-word answer.

In rehab, my voice was taped in the beginning to establish a baseline. *God, is that me? I sound so erratic, stuttering, and complex. It does not make sense. Gibberish!* My ego was completely deflated by the tape recording—not to mention recognition cards. Peggy would hold up a card with a figure on it, and my job was to identify the item. The first time was a total disaster. The card had a pencil on it. I looked at that card for five minutes, my mind totally blank. I recognized it but could not tell you what it was. Peggy pronounced the first syllable and I was still at a loss. The next card had a cat on it; again I failed. Once she told me the answer, I felt like an idiot because I knew what it was the minute she identified it. *Jesus Christ, help me!*

After several weeks I slowly improved. The structure of rehabilitation was consistent: first the line drawing, then the tape recording, and then the card-identification game. I received homework every session. Write five responses for answering the phone. Write five possible answers when asked a question. For example: "Let me get back to you on that," or, "We can talk later," and my favorite, "Excuse me, I will be right back." At the end of six months, I had progressed from drawing a line for each syllable to using my hand to talk. I moved my right hand like I was dusting a table in small strokes, or I cupped my left hand and rubbed it with my right hand for each syllable. Similar to a metronome, this kept a rhythm to my speech. The purpose of using my hand was to keep me focused and speak fluidly. At first, it was awkward and uncomfortable; I focused on moving my hand. My speech was still unnatural—I was looking for words, trying to say a complete sentence. It was choppy. Often I would start the sentence, but halfway through I would have forgotten what I was talking about or I could not remember a word. It was frustrating as hell. My mind was attempting to speak and construct a sentence but then fizzled. I gave up. This was not working. My communication skills were gone. *Who the hell can understand me?*

Four months after my stroke I met with the neurological psychologist. He evaluated my cognitive functions, administering tests over the course of two days to determine the amount of damage. The first day I had to do the identification cards—identify the item on the card and the shapes and geometric test. This included, for example, showing me a triangle with circles and boxes inside. My job was to look at the card and then draw it without looking. This continued for several hours. In the next test, he read a story to me and then listed numbers for me to remember. I would have to recall the details of the story and then the numbers. I was only mildly successful. I recalled three details of the story and only two numbers. I had to repeat this test until I could remember five details and numbers. *God help me, I have no memory functions. How can I return to teaching? What am I going to do? I am so depressed.*

"Today we are going to test your math and comprehension skills." *Oh, terrific!* I needed to match numbers and mathematical symbols within a certain time period. I always hated timed tests. *Could you put any more pressure on me?* There were four separate timed math tests. I took my time focusing on one symbol or number at a time. Unfortunately, they all began to look the same. My mind went totally blank, and I couldn't do anything. *No not now. Come back. Calm down; we can do this.* I was having test anxiety—your mind literally shuts down. I had always felt compassion for my kids who suffered this phobia. The math tests were finished. After the break he administered the comprehension test. The four-page test had words in one column and definitions in the second. My task was to match as many words with their definitions within a certain time period. One hour later, the test time ended. I completed some of the first page and some of the second page. Words such as *calculate, admire, convince,* and *shelter* were devastatingly hard, and finding the definitions was impossible. "I will see you next week with the results." *Don't bother—I already know them. But thank you, anyway.* I met with him the following week. I had diminished skills in most of my cognitive abilities, especially math. *Math? I was an accountant and graded papers. Math? I don't believe this. Give me a break!* "Continue therapy and I will test you again in six months. The brain heals slowly."

Peggy and I met the next day. I burst into her room crying. "It is okay; it has only been a couple of months. The brain takes time to heal," she said. "Frustrated, frustrated, frustrated!" I said as I moved my hand across the table. "Teach yourself the way you taught. Don't give up," she responded. The tape recorder started, and we began our speech rehabilitation. One of my challenges was word finding. I continue to experience trouble finding the right word today. I knew what to say, but I could not always access the right word. It felt like my mind and speech had been short-circuited. Due to the word-finding difficulties, my answers could be vague and incomplete. When under pressure or caught off guard, the inability to respond could become terrifying. A coping skill that I constantly used and still use is moving my hand slowly as a guide to keep focused on the topic of conversation. When I was unable to find the correct word, Peggy told me to slowly explain and describe what I meant. Doing this either helps me think of the word or the person I am speaking with will understand what I am talking about and say the word.

Imagine being a keynote speaker for the first time at a national convention. You have given the same PowerPoint presentation many times to a smaller audience. The night before you practice your presentation in front of the mirror. It is perfect. The next morning you are excited and ready to take on the world. This keynote speech could possibly lead to a promotion or to recognition from your peers. Over a thousand people will be listening to you and your ideas. Finally you are introduced. You walk to the podium, look out at the audience, and suddenly you are unable to say a word. Your throat is in spasm, you become more and more nervous, all the facts are jumbled in your mind, and you cannot say a word. This is similar to what people with aphasia live every day.

The next day I met with my psychologist. I had begun seeing him after my mother's death in 2007. The social studies department chair recommended I see someone. My teaching had not been affected, but my personality had noticeably changed, and the administration and my colleagues were concerned about me. One day on the way home from school I called hospice and asked them if bringing them in had caused my mother to die earlier. I felt responsible for her death. They recommended I meet Dr. Newman. I finally agreed that I should see someone, and the recommendation was all I needed.

Dr. Newman's voice and demeanor were calming and soothing. We spoke in detail about my mother's recent death. I'd felt as though I let her down. I had not done enough to help her. I believed I had brought hospice in too early, and if I had waited, she might still be with us. I regretted that my sisters felt that they were not more involved in her care. We discussed the stages of grieving at our first meeting and scheduled meetings once a week after that. My feelings were normal, he assured me, and he and I would work through the grieving process together. After the stroke, Peggy suggested speaking to my psychologist about my frustration and the depression caused by the stroke. He agreed with Peggy that I needed to use my teaching skills to overcome my problems. "Don't give up. Just do it."

I wanted to go back to my second home, the York Harbor Inn. The hugs, the warm feelings of friendship, the feeling of understanding, and feeling part of the York Harbor Inn family were the emotional medicine I needed. I wanted to go to the outlets and do some shopping. Travel to Wells to the Candy Shoppe to bring back chocolate delights to Paul, Jess, Liam, Sean, Donna, Greg, and the entire family at the Inn. They are wonderful people. The owner is extremely fortunate to have them. They are the Inn; without them it would just be another place to stay in Maine. I yearned for my little corner of the Inn with my water view and deck. Relax, read, and sleep. There I used to ponder on the best way to handle a problem at school, correct papers, and develop curriculum in the community room with its large stone fireplace and roaring fire with unlimited tea or hot chocolate. The Inn had been my retreat for years. The fact that I would be unable drive for another four weeks to my place of tranquility was agonizing. Would I be able to visit again? How would they react to my aphasia and hand movement? *Mother of God, I need to get better!*

My self-teaching adventure commenced. I would continue to do the assignments Peggy gave me, but I also wrote my own curriculum. It was a curriculum similar to the one I had used with my special-education and reading-disabled students. The study in my house was a treasure of old vocabulary books, lower-level reading books, and essay-writing outlines. The first rule of reading is decoding—recognizing a word and understanding its meaning. Vocabulary was to be my initial barrier as well as my speech. I would write the vocabulary word along with the definition and then attempt to say the word using my hand in order to be more fluid when speaking. As a teacher I had always firmly believed that if you write something down, you think and you remember. Dealing with aphasia put this theory to the most important test of my life. While I was teaching, I realized my students did not know how to study because they lacked vocabulary and reading skills. I also realized the more I repeated a story the better the scores. So, as the students entered the classroom every day, I would review the vocabulary. I'd yell out a word and the student would need to give me the definition. If a student did not know it, he or she had to write the word along with the definition five times for homework. Before each test I created a review sheet. We reviewed it in class, and the students had to copy it twice that night and hand it in to me before they took the test the next day. If the student had not completed the assignment, he or she would stay with me that night and write it. The next afternoon he would take the test. Amazingly, the test scores increased by over 27 percent, and the students began using Ms. M.'s theory for their other classes—with positive results. I should mention I never accepted anything printed from a computer—it had to be handwritten. After all, the state assessment exam was all handwritten.

During rehabilitation, I was assessed every two weeks to evaluate my progress in speech, word recognition, reading, and comprehension. My fear of failing (which I did many times) was overwhelming. Assessment is a strain on most students, but for special-needs students it can be hell on earth. Many times I have encountered students who said, "I knew the material, but the minute I received the test, my mind went blank." This is quite common among students. Unfortunately it creates anxiety and hopelessness. How many of us experienced this in our school days? Experiencing this phobia as a student, I created the "round knowledge table" in my class. All students were welcome, especially the special-needs students and reading-disabled students. The table offered them peace of mind. I read the question and the possible answers, observed who was having difficulty, and offered a clue that was given during class. If puzzled faces remained, I simplified and explained the question and possible answers, and if necessary I eliminated one of the answers. It made testing easier and less traumatizing. The open-notebook essay question was assigned on Wednesday based on that week's content, vocabulary, and the notes and essay outline from class. It was due Friday. If a student didn't complete the essay, he or she stayed after school to finish with my help.

Personally, the most severe challenge was my reading and comprehension deficit. Suddenly I could not read, comprehend, or remember anything I read. I was devastated. Decoding, automaticity, word definitions, and phonological awareness were gone. Short-term and long-term memory was nonexistent. I had to start from the beginning. Reading is similar to an internal orchestra. Decoding is the recognition that a group of letters represents a specific word. It is generally recognized that decoding is crucial to comprehension. When the decoding error rate is high, comprehension is low. My first attempt at reading was *I Never Saw Another Butterfly* by Celeste Raspanti, a play. I started reading the play, and one hour later I was only on page eight, could not remember the names of the characters or the plot. I had used this in my classroom for years, and now this!

Frustration, discouragement, and anger flowed through my mind. The next day in rehab I vented my anger. Peggy's response was: "Practice what you teach." That night while reading, I wrote on small four-by-six index cards to guide me through the reading process, trying to meet my needs to decode and comprehend. In school I had used this method called "The Internal Orchestra." The first was decoding—the student underlines words he does not understand, writes the words, finds the definitions and explains them in his own words, then replaces his words in the original writing, which promotes increased understanding. The student can also write clues based on prior knowledge to help him remember the word. Another was character recognition—the student lists each character as he reads. He lists the character's name and who they are, what they did in this chapter, and how they relate to the other characters. Third was comprehension—referring back to the worksheet, the student summarizes the chapter in his own words and personalizes it with a prior-knowledge experience. Before he reads the next chapter, he reviews his previous worksheet as a reminder of what he has read. Fourth, assessment—this process continues for three chapters. After the completion of three chapters, the student is assessed on vocabulary, character information, and comprehension. If he fails the assessment, he returns to the chapter(s) that indicates weakness, and either begins again or modifies the work until mastery of the assessment is met.

Verbal recall and written recall are critical for success. The worksheet will provide the skills of decoding, automaticity, and comprehension. In the beginning, this appears to be difficult, but it does get easier and becomes a compass for reading. Several months later, using the worksheet, I was reading at eighth-grade level. The "Internal Orchestra Worksheet" is simple. It assists in decoding and automaticity and enhances vocabulary and comprehension. My reading skills were improving.

I also worked on my vocabulary. In order for me to say a word, my brain requires me to use a signal or a switch. My signal or coping skill is to move my hand slowly across a table or across my other hand as I verbalize the word. The motion forces me to concentrate or focus on the words I need to have a conversation. If I do not make these movements, I cannot speak.

This method is used to help people who stutter. The stroke affected the left side of my brain, which is the portion of the brain that directs communication, organization, and focus. In my mind, I know what I want to say; however, I cannot verbalize it clearly. I move my hand for two reasons: maintaining focus on my thoughts and speaking with some fluency. Each hand motion represents a syllable of each spoken word. In the beginning, I could only handle one-syllable words, but with time and practice, I am now able to speak fluently. Unfortunately, when I am upset or uncomfortable in a situation, the process tends to go out of sync, and I am unable to express my thoughts. When I am speaking, my word-finding skills diminish, I describe the word to the people I am speaking with, and they in turn will tell me the word. In order to maintain focus and create a sentence, I move my hand for each syllable of each word to create a fluid sentence.

So, starting on page one of an old vocabulary book, I would work on three words. I wrote the words and the definitions, and then I said the words using my hand for guidance many times. The next step was to create a sentence slowly moving my hand. Repeating the sentence and the hand movement slowly increased the fluidity. To be completely truthful, I was ready to give up the first night. As the weeks passed, my speech and hand movement became more in sync. The combination of Peggy's assignments, which were becoming more difficult, and my work at night eventually paid off. Within one year I could have a basic conversation with people. If I lost focus, I would say, "Where was I?" or, "I forgot; what were we talking about?" If I couldn't remember a word, I would describe its function—"You know what I mean: it moves the snow off the street"—and then continue my story.

People's reactions to my aphasia and hand movements are varied. Their body language tells me that people are puzzled as to why I am doing this. Some people look away as I talk or ignore me. Others just lower their eyes and listen. One day I was speaking using my hands (I use the back of my left hand and sweep my right hand across it to speak) in a hardware store. I was looking for a molly screw to hang a heavy picture on a wall. The younger employees had no idea what I was talking about. An older employee became involved and found the screw I was looking for. I said thank you several times. "There is no need to clap," he said. "It is only a screw." I laughed all the way home. Ordering in a restaurant can be interesting. Usually, the person I am dining with will offer to order for me. One day I was in the hospital café after a session with Peggy. I moved my hand across the table and placed my order. The waitress responded, "Don't worry; I just cleaned that table." I explained to her my disability and we both laughed. Manicures are interesting, my manicurist is inquisitive, and to answer her questions, I have to move my hand that is dipped in the soaking water while she is filing my nails on the other hand. Splish splash! I am getting my nails done on a Saturday afternoon.

I worked hard to come back from my stroke and acquire coping skills for my aphasia. I made the choice to work hard and become a person again. This was made more evident to me when the son of my Dad's best friend had a TIA resulting in weakness on one side and a speech problem. He chose to give up. He now lives in a nursing facility. He is fifty-eight years old.

PART THREE

LIFE AFTER MY STROKE

BEGINNING A NEW LIFE

Very few people have a second chance at life. I am a stroke survivor with aphasia. I am different, but I needed the encouragement to move on and continue my ability to learn, grow, and heal. One neurologist told me if my speech did not come back within six months, it would be permanent. My goal was to prove him wrong. I needed positive people around me, pointing me in the direction of healing. My Dad, primary-care doctor, my neurologist, Peggy, and Dr. Newman were my guiding lights. They constantly told me that I can recover my speech and may be able to teach again. They encouraged me with honesty, reminding me that it will not happen all at once, but that it will improve. The body heals with sleep.

We had a family reunion thirteen months after my stroke. I was a bundle of nerves. I had been reclusive due to my speech and hand motion. Very few people had seen me, and I was uncomfortable and embarrassed by my disability. On my weekly visit to Dr. Newman, I mentioned the reunion, crying so hard he could not understand me. Once I quieted down, we calmly discussed how to handle the situation, tears still rolling down my eyes. "People will be caught off guard by your coping skill, but explain to them that you had a stroke and that you use your hand as a metronome to make your speech more fluid. If they react negatively, walk away. You don't need them. Search for people who make you comfortable and stay with them." I was determined to follow his advice. Most people responded graciously but many seemed to show pity. I realized that day that noise can be painful, and that it obstructs my ability to focus and speak. Dr. Newman explained that the noise over-stimulated my brain, causing a temporary inability to concentrate, focus, and speak. What was annoying were the stories I heard about friends who had strokes and are doing really well. "You must be a slow healer. Just try and you will be fine." Comments like that made me scream inside. *What do you think I have been doing for thirteen months? Go to hell.*

My Dad was my backbone throughout rehabilitation. He understood my frustration and helped me communicate. He seemed to know intuitively what I meant when my words were garbled. Although he has always been there for me, unfortunately, he did not encourage me to try teaching again. "You are going to get hurt. You are not able to control your kids like before. You are not up to the stress." Those were some of his comments. My psychologist seemed to agree with my father and expressed concern. "You cannot talk without using your hand; you are making progress, but going back to teaching will not work. You cannot speak clearly under stress. I don't think it is a good idea. You should start writing." My primary-care doctor was encouraging but was afraid of the effects the stress would have on me. "Why don't you try one-on-one teaching or teach with another teacher? That may help you understand what could happen." My colleagues, on the other hand, were encouraging. They believed I was a good teacher and that my problem would take care of itself once I entered the classroom.

The students, they said, needed to be taught tolerance anyway, and working with me would be a great practical lesson.

Throughout my life, my aunt Pat has always been there for me. She is my confidant and friend. *Brilliant* and *comforting* are the words that describe her best. She reminded me that, as a child and as an adult, I always needed a project to work on and complete. She reminded me that as a child I was always knitting, needlepointing, painting, or doing puzzles. As we talked on the phone, we started to reminisce about our vacation to northern New Hampshire in 1997. Visitors would work on the three-thousand-piece puzzle in the community room after the day's activities. As she recalls, I worked on it one night until three o'clock the next morning, and finished it. "You need to find a project to work on," she said. "Start writing curriculum."

Three years after my stroke I decided to prepare to go back to teaching. I had to learn to speak more clearly, create a way to disguise my hand movement, and speak more intelligently. I also had to review or relearn my sophomore social studies curriculum. I searched and finally found a recording of a lecture I had once given in class that I had confiscated from a student. I listened to it and tried to mimic the way I spoke back then, practicing the small and subtle intonations in my voice. God, I wished I had let my students tape my lectures. After several weeks, I realized that my teaching voice was lost forever. I needed to work on a new voice and speech pattern. My voice was not fluid, and that, along with word-loss issues, was not appropriate for classroom teaching. Classroom management, writing on the blackboard, and speaking with my hand were also not the easiest challenges to overcome. I was distraught.

As a teacher, I always told my students to focus on their abilities, and not their disabilities. My abilities were limited; I was relying on the "Mathews effect"—the more you do it, the better you get. Regardless, I needed to return to education or at least contribute to the process. At the time of my stroke, the school where I worked was in the process of revising their scope and sequence. Scope and sequence is a formatted day-by-day curriculum that the teachers are supposed to follow. The purpose is to ensure that teachers in a specific content area are on the same page. I spoke with my department chair, and we agreed it would be a good project for me. The school had created a new format, and my job was to convert the old format to the new format. This was a gift; it introduced me to the educational jargon or buzzwords and aided me in reviewing and reinforcing the content. At first I was overwhelmed, but I practiced what I taught. To scaffold it, I broke it down into smaller tasks. There were six columns to work with, and each column represented a new task. I worked on it for three hours a day and then rested to let my body heal and regenerate. My organizational skills were diminished, and my writing skills were erratic. I finally finished the project four months later with an ecstatic sense of accomplishment. But I also felt inferior because prior to my stroke I would have been able to finish it over a long weekend. But this was my new life, and if things took longer now, then that was okay. The new me was slower, but I got the task done. I reviewed it—modifications were needed big time. Disappointment flowed through every part of my senses. *Calm down, breathe, and continue. You made progress; it just needs a little tweaking.* I made the modifications, proofread it, and sent it to my department head. The problem was that the school had to adopt the federal core standards along with the state standards.

They decided to include the federal core standards in the scope and sequence. Luckily, I was not asked to do it. I suffered a minor TIA after working on revising the scope and sequence I submitted.

I continued my vocabulary and reading every night, with Maggie sitting next to me and Dad watching television. "You will know when you're ready, but you should start driving," he said one night. Another milestone. A few days later, I backed the car out of the garage and drove around the neighborhood. Can you say nervous wreck?

Poststroke issues include the fear it will happen again. These feelings can be devastating: the constant fear that your arm will tingle or a severe headache will debilitate you or that you won't be able to speak again. TIAs can last minutes or hours. They can disable you or have no affect at all other than extreme fatigue. It was time for my annual visit to the neurological psychologist for my two days of tests. I immediately realized I was doing better. I received the result in his office the next week. My long-term and short-term memory was diminished but had improved. My reading and comprehension were only mildly diminished, which was a huge improvement. My focusing and word-finding skills had only slightly improved. Overall there was a mild improvement. These tests indicated that I could no longer teach or work. It had been over two years since the stroke. I was in disbelief. I had done everything I was told to do and then some. What if I worked harder and increased rehabilitation? After all, there was improvement in some tests. The tears I was holding back began to trickle down my face. The neurologist told me I was unable to multitask and my memory deficits along with my aphasia would make it impossible to teach again. *What am I suppose to do? Sit home and watch television all day? I don't think so!*

The following day, Dr. Newman and I discussed the probability of me going back to teaching. We agreed that my physical and cognitive disabilities were not the characteristics of a typical good teacher. Teaching requires multitasking. Classroom management requires constant supervision, while at the same time teaching your lesson for the day. Writing notes on the blackboard, checking to be sure the special-education students are not having difficulties, and watching for any signs of trouble before they escalate—those are just a few of the duties a teacher has to perform. Needing your hand to talk can be a distraction and a sign of weakness, which troublemakers might try to use to their advantage. No, teaching was not an option.

I was devastated. Something had died in me. I had several minor TIAs since the stroke, causing hospitalization for several days. Each time my speech would regress but thankfully would come back to baseline within a few days. Adding this to the other issues I'd have if I went back to teaching, it was the deal breaker. The students would be at risk if I had another TIA. The decision had already been made immediately after the stroke, but I had disagreed. I was just yearning to go back, but realized that I couldn't. The grieving process began.

The vocational technical school was always very generous to me. I had taken time off on the Federal Family Leave Act when my mom was sick. After I had the stroke, I applied for sick days through the sick bank, which allowed me to be paid. When those days were drained, I applied for and was granted an unpaid leave of absence. During the 2011–2012 school year, I was refused another request for unpaid leave of absence. I was under the delusion that I could teach with just a little more time. My stubbornness and perseverance had never let me down before. Maybe the doctors were overreacting? All I wanted was to be with my kids! In August 2011, I went to school for a meeting with the superintendent to discuss my future at the school. I had not been in the school since the stroke, and I was overwhelmed with emotions upon entering the building. The dean of discipline, my protector, was unbelievably understanding of my disability. Then I met with the superintendent, and we discussed my future. She watched my hand as I spoke, and suddenly bombarded me with questions. My brain became overwhelmed; my speech process went out of sync. I could not put a response together. I could not answer her in complete sentences, and then the worst-case scenario occurred: my coping skills for my aphasia became still—my hand would not move. This had never happened before. I was so overwhelmed that my thought process abandoned me. I was nervous, angry, and unable to get it together. My mind shut down. I was in the same place I was after the stroke—the first day of rehab. *What just happened?* I sat there unable to speak clearly, barely able to hold back my tears. The superintendent's response was: "The meeting is over." The next day I e-mailed her, asking for another appointment. We agreed to meet in September.

The September meeting went as expected. I told her I wanted a trial experiment to determine if I was capable to teach again. I volunteered to sit in a classroom with a veteran teacher and offer guidance to the special-education and reading-disabled students. She refused. I volunteered to be a paraprofessional with one-on-one interaction with a student. She refused. I reiterated it was only a trial and pleaded with her to give me a chance. She refused. "Your hand movement is a distraction.

Our prior meeting illustrated your reaction under pressure. I am sorry. You are dismissed, a.k.a. terminated." What about teaching children tolerance for the disabled? You know, I am very good with special-education and reading-disabled children. I requested a letter of recommendation and thanked her for her time. I left the building devastated. Reality had slapped me in the face. It was true I could never teach again. Everyone had been right. My psychologist, my father, and my primary-care physician had known what they were talking about: going back to teaching was a bad idea. Several days later, I went to the York Harbor Inn to reflect on my stroke, my rehabilitation, and my goals. I realized my perseverance was not going to help me this time. It was time to give up my goal to go back to teaching. Realizing that my goal was unreachable was a milestone in my recovery as I grieved, let it go, and moved on. But to what? I felt like a lost soul.

WRITING JOURNEY

In 2007, several days before my mother died, hospice told me to stop her injections. I refused. They always seemed to help her. The hospice nurse called the oncologist, and he spoke with me. "Carol, it is over. The medication will not work. You and your father kept her alive three years longer than anyone expected. But now it is over. Let her go. Help her by letting her die in peace. You need to go back to living." I was devastated. At the same time, I realized I had been in denial for a long time. My grieving process began. Back then, however, I had a place to go during the process. My kids at school were waiting for me. I established a college scholarship in her name for special-needs and reading-disabled children.

This time, however, I had no place to return to. I needed to realize that I could not teach anymore, but without an alternative plan, this was a hard blow. Denial is part of the grieving process, but eventually you have to move beyond that. Finally accepting my new reality meant that my true recovery and new journey were about to begin. After long discussions, Dr. Newman and I decided that writing would be my connection to education. My other confidants and doctors agreed. During rehabilitation, I had begun to realize how a special-education and reading-disabled student must feel in the classroom. I had a rare opportunity to see both sides. Reflecting on my teaching years, I thought about the many special-education and reading-disabled students I taught. I wrote curriculum specifically for them. I remembered how *I Never Saw Another Butterfly* written by Celeste Raspanti was the hallmark curriculum for my kids. There is no question on the English language arts state assessment this play cannot answer. We used to read the play in class—each student had a role to play. I remembered writing previous state questions on the blackboard, and writing the essays with them. One of the funniest moments occurred on the day of the exam. I walked into my classroom to collect papers that needed to be graded. The test administrator called me over and asked me why the state assessment essay question was on the blackboard with an outline. "What?" I said. "We were practicing writing essays, and I randomly picked that one." I was shocked. "Well, erase it," he responded. "Yes, sir!" That day every one of my kids came in to tell me I was psychic and that they wrote the same essay they had written the day before in class. "You are great, Ms. M.! Scary but great."

I remember that every January I would spend a week asking my students what they were interested in or what book they would like to read for me. Each class made its own list. I would check the reading level to be sure it was in range. When this task was completed, I announced I had ordered and paid for their books from Barnes & Noble. The doubting Thomases wanted to see the receipt, which I showed them. "I care for you enough to buy you the book. In return all you have to do is read it and write an MCAS-quality essay." I was making out on the deal. They read their books, used the essay outlines I provided, and after February vacation, I received all three hundred essays.

Friday was set aside to correct and edit them until they were MCAS quality, so they'd receive a high school diploma. Ah, those were the good old days.

My aunt Pat suggested I write about my teaching experiences, and so my writing journey began. One of the themes of *ASCD Express*, an educational journal, was improving reading skills. Bingo! This was my former forte, and I figured I could probably submit an article. Enthusiasm came and then vanished. *I don't remember how to write an article; where do I start? What is the format? I know the information, but how do I put it together?* Aunt Pat suggested I e-mail or call them to send the format and necessary information. Duh, why didn't I think of that? I started my article "A Stroke, a Blessing, a New Insight." I wrote my outline and thoughts over a period of five days. Then I started writing, and then I cried. Every sentence I wrote, I immediately repeated in the next line. Every sentence I wrote, I immediately repeated in the next line. I was dumbstruck. According to the doctor, that was the way my mind worked, especially when I speak. Dr. Newman suggested a piece of equipment that I could speak into and the computer would write the words for me. Actually, it worked pretty well, except it picked up my speech repetition, and I despised listening to my voice. But I kept at it, because with a published article I could influence education with my new perspective on teaching special-education and reading-disabled students.

Three years after the stroke I was driving again and decided to visit my second home, the York Harbor Inn. The warm greetings and hugs were welcomed. I walked into my room and there were flowers, candy, and cards welcoming me home. I explained why I moved my hand, and their reaction was, "Who cares?" and "I didn't even notice." Life was good. I started my article, ignoring the repetition. The staff solved my word-loss issues. I would go out to the front desk and describe the word I was looking for, and eventually someone would think of it. I included my strategies and worksheets I used when I was learning to read again. Once again, I referred to the "Matthew's Effect": the more you do it, the better you get. After editing all my repetitive lines, I sent it to my uncle Carl, a former English teacher, for his opinion and comments. He made his edits, and then I sent it to *ASCD Express* for review and possible publication. Ten months later the article was published. I cannot express how ecstatic I felt. I had done something that made me feel functional and meaningful. My writing career had begun. It was an unbelievable feeling. I had found my place in life. I was a writer. Wow!

A professor at Rivier University read the article and asked me to create a PowerPoint presentation for her graduate students in education. The presentation went well. I used my coping skills for the most part, but at one point decided to illustrate aphasia. I sat on my hands and attempted to speak about the importance of understanding the mind of a special-education student. After a while I restarted my coping skills. I had not known that it takes a few minutes to return to fluidity. Everyone in the lecture hall was tearful, including me. I had put myself in an extremely vulnerable position, because the experience took me back to my condition right after my stroke. It was an intense moment, but I felt it was necessary to illustrate the aphasia, and to provide the graduate students with an insight into the mind of a special-education student, complete with the lack of focus, a mind buzzing at warp speed, and the inability to answer question without enough time. Life can be difficult, but it is how you handle this difficulty that can make a world of difference.

Currently I am writing for Stroke-Network.com, a creative and innovative online information center for people who have experienced strokes. People read stories of hope from other stroke victims. Doctors make suggestions and discuss new research being done. At the moment, I am working on a series of articles on caregiving. It still takes me three times as long to write now than it did before the stroke, and I still repeat every sentence; but things could have been a lot worse. It is a nuisance, but, considering the alternative, I can handle it.

The stroke was a blessing for me. It illustrated the power of hard work and the need for more patience. It taught me the healing power of sleep. It also taught me the power I have inside—the power to make my own decisions, to let go of the past, and to live life by making choices that enhance me and my interest. I have learned that the past can only be relived in your mind. The choice to relive those painful memories is your decision. Let them go, and your life can be filled with happiness and new experiences. Forgive yourself for prior mistakes and let others choose to forgive you. If they don't forgive you, accept it and move on. Do not dwell on it; move on. I have made many mistakes in my life. I apologized, but in some cases, I was not forgiven. My new life has given me the chance to accept that and move on. Accept that everyone has their own issues to deal with and that these issues are not yours. Letting go is one of the hardest things to do, but it is worth it. Your health and your life will improve. The stroke made me realize that I have the power to stop pondering or thinking about past events and to consciously realign myself to the present and a new life. The aphasia has helped me avoid hostile or uncomfortable situations, simply because I am incapable of handling them. Why bother getting upset or emotional when you can just as easily walk away?

The stroke and aphasia also gave me an opportunity to change some of my less appealing personality traits: stubbornness and arrogance, sarcasm, and my sometimes intimidating behavior. I made a choice not to allow these characteristics to be part of me again. They produce painful memories, which I'd rather forget. Life is too short. I will never be the same, but in some ways, this is a good thing. Out with the old and in with the new. Since the stroke, I have found a new life; I am making new memories with friends and I am enjoying myself immensely. I have set up and maintained barriers that help me avoid anything or anyone out of my comfort zone.

Please take control of your health and life. Take control over the power you possess in your brain. Eat healthy, exercise, and listen to your body. If it is tired, allow the healing power of sleep to care for it. You have to choose to live happily or to live with outside nocuous interference. You should find the balance, or chi, as the Chinese call it. Believe me: it can make a world of difference to your health and mind. As I always told my students: "Treat people the way you want to be treated, and you will seldom have a problem."

LIFESAVING SIGNS OF A STROKE

Please do not ignore any of these signs. Call 911 or the Fire Department immediately.

It could save your life or save you from residual effects of a stroke.

Symptoms of stroke are
- sudden numbness or weakness of the face, arm, or leg (especially on one side of the body)
- sudden confusion or trouble speaking or understanding speech
- sudden trouble seeing in one or both eyes, sudden trouble walking, dizziness, or loss of balance or coordination
- sudden severe headache with no known cause

RESOURCES

American Stroke Association
National Center
7272 Greenville Avenue
Dallas, Texas 75231
Toll-Free: 1-888-4-STROKE
www.strokeassociation.org

American Speech-Language Hearing Association
2200 Research Boulevard
Rockville, MD 20850
Phone: 1-800-638-8255
actioncenter@asha.org
www.asha.org

National Aphasia Association
350 Seventh Avenue
Suite 902
New York, NY 10001
Phone: 1-212-267-2814
Phone: 1-800-922-4NAA (4622)
naa@aphasia.org
www.aphasia.org

Carol M. Maloney

Aphasia Hope Foundation
2436 West 137th Street
Leawood, KS 66224
Phone: 1-913-402-8306
www.aphasiahope.org

CPSIA information can be obtained at www.ICGtesting.com
Printed in the USA
BVOW04s1454021013

332634BV00003B/237/P